Echoes Of Me

Poetic Reflections of Life and Beyond

Divya Ashok

BookLeaf Publishing

India | USA | UK

Made with ❤ on the BookLeaf Publishing Platform
www.bookleafpub.in
www.bookleafpub.com

Dedication

To all those who seek solace and beauty in the embrace of nature.

Preface

"Echoes of Me: Poetic Reflections of Life and Beyond" was born out of deep connection to the natural world. These poems are reflections of my voice in my mind. You may find peace, nature, music, life, passion, beauty and simple moments that the earth offers. This collection is a celebration of the timeless bond between humanity and nature.

Acknowledgements

Heartfelt gratitude to the natural world for being an endless source of inspiration. Special thanks to my readers, whose love for poetry makes this journey worthwhile. Your support and appreciation are deeply valued.

1. The Thief called Time

Time is a thief, so silent, so sly.
Stealing our moments as days pass by.
It takes our laughter, our yesterdays
bright,
Leaving behind just whispers at night.

The echoes fade, the faces blur,
Memories slip like wind through fur.
No hands can halt, no heart can plead,
Time marches on with restless speed.

So, hold each second, make it shine,
Let love and joy in moments twine.
For though we can't command its flow,
We chose how bright our days will glow.

2. My First Love: Teaching

Since I was small, I used to play,
With chalk and board almost every day.
Not doctor, not pilot – I always knew,
A teacher's path was mine to pursue.

She walked in grace, my role model dear,
Her words still echo in my ear.
I watched, I learned, I found my light,
And dreamed of classrooms every night.

Others had plans, but I held on tight,
To my little dream, burning bright.
Teaching, not just what i do,
It's the soul of me, honest and true.

3. Economics: The Hidden Pulse

No one knows what economics means,
They think it's charts and money scenes.
But it's the way we spend and save,
The choices that we make and crave.

From morning tea to market run,
Economics hides in everyone.
It's how we share, how prices grow,
It's all around, more than we know.

It shapes our world, both big and small,
In homes, in shops, in every call.
It's not just books, it's how we live,
A silent guide in what we give.

4. A Mother's 'me' Time

She wakes before the sun can rise,
With sleep still resting in her eyes.
She packs, she cooks, she runs around,
But in her world, she's rarely found.

A fruit in her hand, but not for her,
She gives it with a loving stir.
Their health, their joy – she puts first,
Even when her own needs thirst.

But mothers too deserve some space,
A quiet sip, a slower pace.
Her health is gold, her peace is key,
Let her rest, let her just be.

So dear family, lend your grace,
Give her time, give her place.
Not just a mom – she's someone too,
Who needs a little care from you.

5. Reels And the Lost Real

Once they called the TV an idiot box,
But we still ran barefoot on dusty rocks.
We played outside till the evening bell,
With scraped knees and stories to tell.

We feared our elders, showed respect,
Waited our turn, learned to reflect.
There was patience in the way we grew,
And life felt rich in all we knew.

But now it's screens, endless scrolls,
Reels that steal the days and souls.
No sky gazing, no muddy feet,
Just flashing lights and a tapping beat.

Dear children, pause – just lift your eyes,
There's magic still in earth and skies.
Don't miss the life that nature weaves,
It's worth much more than hearts and feeds.

6. Knowledge with Wisdom

We may read and learn for years,
Fill our minds and clear our tears.
But without wisdom by our side,
Even knowledge loses pride.

A handful of sand, that's all we know,
While the ocean of truth continues to flow.
It's not the loud who truly see,
But the quiet minds who choose to be.

The wise don't shout, they stop and see,
They learn from ants, from sky, from tree.
Even a child can teach us more,
If we keep ego at the door.

So let your mind stay open wide,
With learning, walk in grace and pride.
The more you know, the more you bend,
Be humble, kind, a thoughtful friend.

7. My Father, My Forever Light

You left too soon, but left so much,
Your words, your grace, your gentle touch.
A man of discipline, strong and wise,
With dreams that reached beyond the skies.

You gave us books, you gave us light,
Taught us to choose what's true and right.
"Don't chase money", you used to say,
"Grow with pride in an honest way".

Your presence carried a quiet charm,
A silent strength, a steady calm.
And though you're gone, I feel you nearby,
In every step, in every tear.

I saw that pride shine in your eye,
The day I soared, the day I tried.
That moment lives, inside of me-
My crown, my memory, endlessly.

8. Rain, Tea and Laughter

A cup of tea, the window wide,
The clouds come in; the sun must hide.
The breeze is soft, the earth smells sweet,
As raindrops tap in gentle beat.

The world turns calm, the sky turns grey,
But joy and peace both find their way.
Beside me sits my laughing brother,
We joke and smile like no other.

No rush, no race, just little things-
Like muddy air and clouded wings.
My heart feels full, my soul feels free,
In rain, in tea, in family.

9. Let's Help Our Earth

The trees are gone, the water's low,
The dirty smoke begins to grow.
The sea is filled with plastic waste,
And fish are dying in their haste.

The earth is tired, but still she gives,
She keeps us safe; she helps us live.
She takes our harm, she takes our pain,
And still, she sends the sun and rain.

Let's keep her clean, let's keep her green,
Let's teach our kids what nature means.
So, they can grow and help her too,
And build a world that's kind and true.

10. Morning Jewels

The morning breeze is cold and sweet,
The rising sun begins to greet.
The flowers wear small drops of dew,
Like tiny jewels, fresh and new.

Some shine like stars, some look like
Glass,
They sparkle bright as moments pass.
They sit on leaves and softly stay,
Then slowly fade with light of day.

The dew drops kiss the morning green,
A lovely sight, so calm, so clean.
Nature's gift in morning light-
Soft and pure and shining bright.

11. Moon In the Night

The night is quiet, calm and still,
The moon shines bright beyond the hill.
She looks so lovely in the sky,
Like a queen who watches from up high.

The stars around her shine so small,
But she still glows and lights up all.
Children laugh and run below,
Playing in her silver glow.

Poets write and lovers' dream,
The moon lights up their every theme.
She is our earth's bright, glowing light-
A gift of peace in every night.

12. Grandma's Saree

Grandma's saree, so old and pure,
Feels like holding a tale so sure.
A piece of history soft and deep,
She kept it safe for me to keep.

It smells like pages of a classic book,
With pride and care, I looked.
No modern silk, none shined so bright,
Can match her saree's gentle light.

She wore it once with power and grace,
A queen in every move and pace.
When I draped it around my frame,
A trace of boldness in me came.

13. She is Strong

She wakes up strong each day,
No matter what comes her way.
She smiles through pain and fear,
And keeps her loved ones nearby.

She tries, she fails, she stands,
With dreams held in her hands.
She doesn't run from night,
She walks with quiet light.

She works, she loves, she gives,
In every heart, she lives.
She turns her tears to gold,
Her courage bright and bold.

She may be soft and kind,
But strength is in her mind.

14. Salute to the Soldier

While we sleep in peace each night,
They stand guard in cold and fight.
Through rain and snow, through heat and pain,
They hold the line, again and again.

Not for fame, not for praise,
They live in silence, brave always.
Their hearts beat for the tricolor high,
Even if it means they say goodbye.
They have families, dreams and fears,
But wipe them off with no more tears.
For every breath we take so free,
A soldier paid the price, silently.

True patriotism wears no show–
It lives where our soldiers go.
To each brave soul who stands so tall,
We salute you, one and all.

15. The Lazy Age

One button starts the fan and light,
No need to move, no strength, no fight.
Just say a word, things come alive,
We barely walk yet hope to thrive.

We sit all day, we barely play,
Our bodies slow, they waste away.
Phones and screens have made us blind,
To real joy, to our own mind.

No need to grind, no need to try,
Just gadgets there for every why.
Be as we rest, we slowly fade,
And lose the life our elders made.

Where is the spark, the work, the flame?
Without it, life won't feel the same.

16. The Magic of Music

Music flows like morning light,
Filling hearts, making things right.
A tune, a beat, a voice so true,
Can chase away the darkest blue.

It lifts us up, it calms us down,
Wipes away each worry's frown.
It's joy, it's hope, it's fire and peace,
In every note, our fears release.

No pill, no cure, no spoken line,
Can heal the soul the way songs shine.
It dances in the heart so free,
A timeless, tender melody.

From pain to power, dull to bright-
Music turns the dark to light.

17. I Still Rise

I was hurt when I was small,
Too afraid to speak at all.
The world felt heavy, cold and wide,
So, I kept everything inside

But slowly I began to grow,
Found my voice and let it show.
The fear is there, but now I fight,
I walk with strength into the light.
I may be bruised, but I'm not weak,
I've learned to stand, I've learned to speak.
From a quiet child to someone wise-
I found myself... and still I rise.

18. Money and Happiness

Money can buy a bed, not sleep,
A watch for time, but not what's deep.
It fills your hands, but not your heart,
It builds a life – but just one part.

It brings some joy, it lights the way,
But can't replace a warm "okay".
True smiles are free, pure love is gold,
Not everything is bought or sold.

So, earn with grace, but don't forget,
The richest hearts are not in debt.
In the end, what matters most -
Is peace within, not what you boast.

19. The Hands That Raised You

Don't forget the hands so true,
That held you close and carried you.
They fed you food, they wiped your tears,
Ans stayed beside you through the years.

They worked so hard without a rest,
And always gave you all the best.
They cheered you on, they let you grow,
Their silent love you may not know.

You may go far, you may shine bright,
But think of them each day and night.
For all you are, and all you do -
Begins with hands that lifted you.

20. With Discipline, The World is Yours

Wake up with purpose, rise with grace,
Let discipline guide your every pace.
Not every day will feel like gold,
But steady steps will make you bold.

No magic trick, no sudden win,
Just quiet strength that burns within.
The one who stays when others fall,
Will one day rise above them all.

Dreams are seeds, but effort grows -
A life of beauty only effort knows.
So, sharpen your will, and close the doors,
To doubt – with discipline, the world is yours.

21. Rise and Reign

When you have nothing, not even a way,
Let your will be the light that carves your day.
No gold, no guide, no hand to hold -
Still walk like your heart is bold.

Every step in dust, every tear you hide,
Builds the strength that lives inside.
You don't need riches to start the climb.
Just faith that whispers, "It's your time".

And when you rise, when crowns are nearby,
Wear success without pride or fear.
Let your attitude speak, calm and true -
Not louder, just deeper than they knew.

For real power isn't loud or wild,
It's the quiet strength of a once - lost child.

www.ingramcontent.com/pod-product-compliance
Lightning Source LLC
LaVergne TN
LVHW021358200726
843509LV00014B/2912